ANCIENT GREECE
for
CHILDREN

by

John Richardson

Illustrated by

Robbie Peterson

Copyright

ISBN 978-1-4709-4925-9

9 781470 949259

Dedication

To my family who travelled with me to see many of the wonders of Ancient Greece.

For children everywhere to enjoy reading and learning about history.

Other publications by John Richardson

For teenagers and adults:

The Romans and The Antonine Wall of Scotland
- ISBN 9-780244-502935

In Search of Agricola
- ISBN 9-781008-981669

Roman Britain for Children
- ISBN 9-781794-843196

Index

INTRODUCING ELENA

Hello, my name is Elena. I'm going to tell you about the history of Ancient Greece, Athens and Sparta.

Two thousand five hundred years ago, Ancient Greece was one of the most important regions in the world. The Greeks had many famous artists, actors, builders and athletes participating in different sports. One famous Greek thinker was named Plato, who wrote down his thoughts in books called "dialogues". He is still considered one of the world's greatest thinkers today.

The people of Greece lived on the land, along the coast, and also on the many Islands in the Mediterranean Sea. They called themselves Hellenes and their land Hellas. When the Romans arrived in our country, they named it Greece.

Can you answer the questions Elena asks you throughout the book? The answer can be found on the page of her question.

A LONG TIME AGO

Some three thousand years ago, Greece was already a very ancient land. People have lived in this land for a very long time. It was and still is a very warm country during the summer. It became one of the most advanced civilisations in the ancient world.

They brought their Alphabet to Europe as well as their many books, which we still read and study today. The Greeks were the first people to create what we call Politics, and they studied the Stars and Science. They went to watch plays at their theatres.

But the peoples of Ancient Greece were not just one people. They lived in many city-states.

These states were protected by the most powerful City States like Athens and Sparta.

Sometimes even those City States would not agree with each other, so wars among them happened quite often.

Elena: *"Can you name two of the powerful city States?"*

WHAT CLOTHES WERE WORN

Because Ancient Greece was such a warm country, the men, women and children wore garments that kept them cool. Tunics were loose-fitting, which allowed the heat to escape from their warm bodies.

Men wore both tunics that could be short or long, and even wore cloaks.

Women and men held tunics in place with pins at their shoulders. The Greeks called these chitons. Around their waists, they wore a belt often made of fabric.

When going outdoors, women would protect their heads and hair from the hot sun and wear Sunhats. Rich ladies would wear jewellery made from Gold, like rings, necklaces and decorated pins for their cloaks. In Ancient Greece, men wore fashionable beards, which they kept neatly trimmed.

Elena: *"What jewellery did rich ladies wear?"*

PARTY TIMES

In Ancient Greece, celebrations were mostly for men. Women and children had their own separate celebrations. The men would play a number of games. One very messy game involved throwing cups of wine at a target. If they missed, they had to drink more wine. It was the job of slaves to wash the hands and the feet of guests. Sometimes even slave children would do this. Food was served, and this could be fish as they lived near the sea, meat with different vegetables followed by cakes and fruit. Parties could last for hours, with guests eating and drinking and talking about their jobs and friends. Musicians played music to help entertain the guests. The flute was one instrument the Greeks enjoyed playing and listening to.

Elena: *"What was one type of instrument the musicians played?"*

AT THE MARKET

In nearly every Greek town and city, there was a market square which would be a very busy place. People would walk around and talk to friends about everyday things and what they hoped to buy that day. There were many stalls with a choice of goods sold by traders from all over Greece. Artisans sold different goods, which included pots made from clay in their workshops.

At some markets, a raised platform could be found on which slaves were paraded, waiting to be sold to wealthy Greeks. The Greeks already paid by using coins made from silver.

Elena: *"What were the slaves standing on at the market?"*

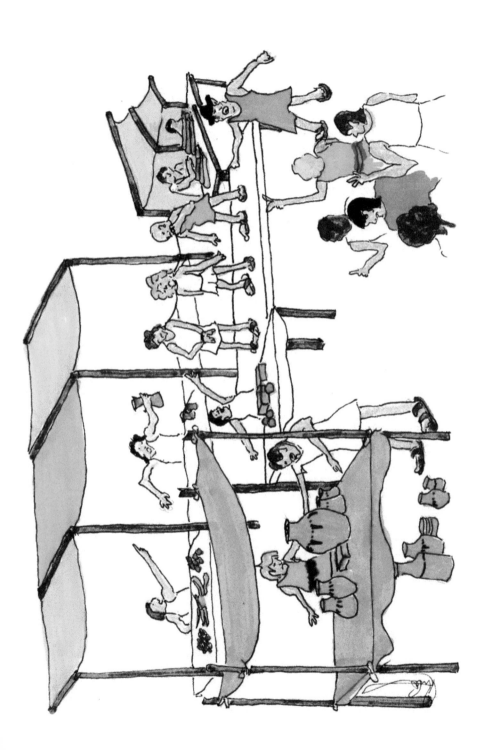

HOUSES IN ANCIENT GREECE

Not all the people lived in the towns and cities. Some lived in the spacious and peaceful countryside. The houses were not unlike today, with two floors. The way they lived was slightly different, though. Men usually lived in their own rooms inside the house on the ground floor, while the women had their rooms on the top floor of the house. Children would also usually be with the women. The temples in the towns and cities were built on high ground so everyone could see them. Ancient Greek houses were built by using both wood and bricks made of clay mud baked in the hot sun or using kilns. Wealthy house owners would have slaves and children helping them to do all the work needed to keep the house clean.

Elena: *"What types of materials did the Greeks use to build their houses?"*

MYTHS AND MONSTERS

As Greek children, we were told about both the awful monsters that lived as well as the brave heroes that fought them. There were many monsters, but one of the most fearsome was Medusa. It was said that if anybody even glanced at her, she turned them into stone, like a statue. The hero who decided to end stop this terrible monster once and for all was Perseus, a strong and intelligent man. He made his plan to destroy her. He looked for her in the hills, and to avoid having to look at her; he carried with him a brass shield. He had polished his shield so that it shone like a mirror. By not looking at Medusa directly and by using the reflection of his shield, he was able to cut off the monster's head. When he returned to his people, his adventure was told all over Greece, and he became a famous hero. Ancient Greece had many heroes. A lion-fighting hero was named Hercules. Hercules also had many adventures and sailed the seas with Jason and the Argonauts, looking for monsters and killing them if they could.

Elena: *"Who was the Hero that cut off the head of Medusa?"*

GOING TO THE THEATRE

Just like people today, the Greeks enjoyed going to their local theatre. The theatres, however, were outside. Open-air theatres were much more conformable during the hot summers. They were built in very large semi-circles, often set on a hillside. All the seats were made of stone, so people would sit on padded cushions.
The seating was arranged so everyone could see the actors perform on the stage.
A wore different masks, which portrayed the characters being performed in the play. The plays were either funny or sad. Women were not yet allowed to act on stage. The stage was for men only.

Elena: *"What was the shape of the theatres built on the hillsides?"*

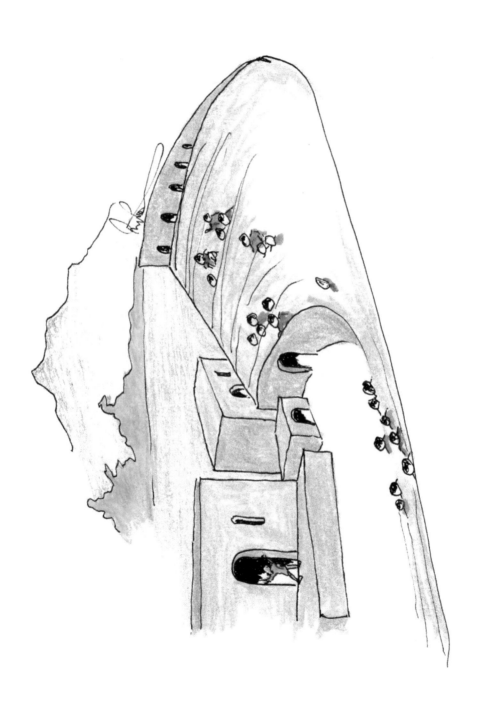

GODS AND GODDESSES

In ancient Greece, it was thought most important to listen and talk to the Greek Gods and Goddesses. In the city of Athens, people would come from the towns and villages to visit temples and worship Gods such as Apollo, Zeus and Athena. People also went to their local temples to talk and pray to the Gods. The temples held many wonderful statues, which helped the people focus as they stood before them, asking for their help. Both Priests and Priestesses communicated with the Gods and would then advise the visiting people. The Ancient Greeks celebrated the Gods with arranged festivals throughout the year. These festivals included processions, dancing and music. They would sometimes last for many days as people enjoyed themselves.

One important Goddess was named Nike and had wings. She was seen as a provider of good luck and victories. One of her statues can be seen today in the Louvre museum in Paris.

Elena: *"Who talked to the Gods inside the temples?"*

OLYMPIC GAMES

The Olympic Games were held every four years.
But there were many games just like them all over
Greece and for many reasons. Even with funerals,
people organised competitive sports events. One
of the most popular sports was running. Other
sports were the long jump,
boxing and wrestling. Throwing the discus was also
popular. Just like today, people trained hard and
could get injuries.
Winning made athletes heroes in their towns,
village or city. For those who lost, it was
sometimes seen as a disgrace or embarrassment.
People also liked chariot races, where horses
would run around a circuit with the driver
standing in the chariot.

Elena: *"Which sport is mentioned*
that included the help of
animals?"

GREEK HEROES

In Ancient Greece, heroes were believed to be more than just mere mortals. Something that heroes often had in common was that one of their parents was a God. They had incredible strength and many skills and were blessed with intelligence. This gave them the power to solve problems that were very difficult for mortals. Therefore the help of heroes was often needed. There were many heroes, like Hercules and Achilles, who helped people. Achilles was one of the Greeks' greatest heroes and fought in the famous Trojan War. His mother held him in the river named Styx by his heel, which made him immortal. His heel, however, not having touched the water, became his weakness. This is why the tendon in your heel is named after Achilles. Heroes were all blessed by the Gods for their great strength and courage when having to face dangers.

Elena: *"Can you find the names of two great Greek heroes?"*

WOMEN AND CHILDREN

In Ancient Greece, having children was considered very important for the future family. To help women become great mothers, they were encouraged to take part in sacred rituals which would help them become fertile and have children. One such famous and important ritual was called the festival of Thesmophoria. Only the women who were married could take part in this festival. Children were important for both the home and the city they grew up in.

If parents were unable to have children, their wealth and property could not be passed on. In Ancient Greece, children and the status they gave their parents were very important in this complex society.

Elena: *"What was the name of the important festival?"*

BOYS IN SPARTA

Children who lived in Sparta were treated differently from children who lived in other parts of Greece. When a baby boy was born, soldiers from the Spartan Amy would come to the home to see if the baby would grow up a strong child. They carried out bathing the child in wine instead of water. If they thought the baby was weak, the soldiers took it away and left it on a hillside or if lucky; it would become a slave.

Parents did not decide on the life of the baby. It was the city-state that made these decisions. When the child reached seven years of age, he or she was taken away and trained to be a soldier. They had to endure physical pain and show endurance, and had to follow the Spartan Warrior code. To become citizens at the age of 20, they had to pass many hard tests. Many never became full citizens of Sparta. At the age of 30, they could return home and live with their parents but continued to train as a warrior until they were 60, when they could retire.

Elena: *"Can you tell me at what age boys could become citizens?"*

30

GIRLS IN SPARTA

Just like the Spartan men, women were expected to be very fit and had to take part in physical exercise. They had to learn how to ride on horses, taught to wrestle, run and throw the disc and spear. This meant they could compete in women-only games and face any challenge. Their fitness meant they could have healthy children and also fight to protect their homes when the men were away.

Girls and Boys were separated when they reached the age of 7 years. Girls stayed at home until they were 18 years of age. The Spartans believed that this was a good age to start having babies.

Women in Sparta wore short dresses which were open on the sides, which made moving around much easier. In Sparta, the women were freer and more powerful than in the rest of Greece. Especially when compared to the women living in Athens.

Elena: *"Until what age did Spartan girls stay at home?"*

BOYS IN ATHENS

In ancient Athens, it was the practice for boys to drink wine, and they would go to school at the age of 7 years. Their teachers taught them math and how to read and write. Physical exercise was also seen as very important for boys. They practised sports like swimming, wrestling and archery. If the boy came from a wealthy family, he also learned about horses and how to ride. When they reached the age of 18, boys would attend military school so they could become good soldiers for Athens. Books were expensive, so reading and writing were done on wax tablets. They would also have to study the words written by the famous poet Homer. If they liked music, they could be taught how to play the lyre or another instrument.
By the age of 30, they would marry and enter into politics.

Elena: *"What school would they attend when they were 18 years of age?"*

GIRLS IN ATHENS

Many women in ancient Athens were able to read and write as well. Some could also play music on an instrument. But unlike women in Sparta, they had few choices on what they could do.
They were able to own slaves who would help them run the household. But they could not vote or own valuable objects. If they spoke badly to their husband, they could be beaten or locked up in their own house. They faced many restrictions in their lives. Girls in ancient Athens stayed at home with their mothers until they married. It was their father who picked the man they married. Nearly everything in a girl's life was decided by the father. If they married, they could not return home, and it was nearly impossible to get a divorce from a bad husband.
When they started their own household after marriage, they would be taught how to run a home. From a young age, they already learned to care for younger children, cook and mend clothes. However, girls could attend festivals and visit neighbours. They could also learn how to sing and dance and play an instrument

Elena: *"Who was the person deciding most everything for girls?"*

NEWBORN INFANTS

When a child was born in ancient Greece, the family would hang a wreath above the door for a boy and wool for a girl. On the fifth day, the family would celebrate with a ceremony and a feast known as the Amphidromia. This was their way to officially welcome into the family the New Born. The child would be given a name, and if this was for a boy, an olive branch was shown outside of the home.

In ancient Rome, they would celebrate a new birth with a ceremony they called the *Lustratio*. This took place nine days after the child was born. The family made offerings to the Gods, and again the parents put on a feast, and the newborn would be shown to the guests. Both the ancient Greeks and ancient Romans thought that childbirth was only the business of women, and so they had only midwives attend to the birth of newborn infants.

Elena: *"What day did the ancient Greeks celebrate the New Born?"*

GREEK SHIPS

There were two basic types of ships used by the Greeks. One was built for trade and carrying goods, and the other was built for soldiers to keep the seas around Greece safe. It was called a trireme which had three rows of sailors on each side holding an oar to row with. These ships also had large brass rams, which would make holes in a ship of the enemy. Both these ships did not just have rowers but also large sails. Athens had the best boats and sailors. The Greeks used their ships often as this was the best way of moving around in a country with many islands and surrounded by sea. Sparta, on the other hand, did not have many boats and was known best for their fearsome warriors who mainly travelled by land.
Before Greek sailors left the safety of the land, they would offer their prayers to the sea god Poseidon and seek his protection.

Elena: *"Who was the Sea God that sailors would pray to?"*

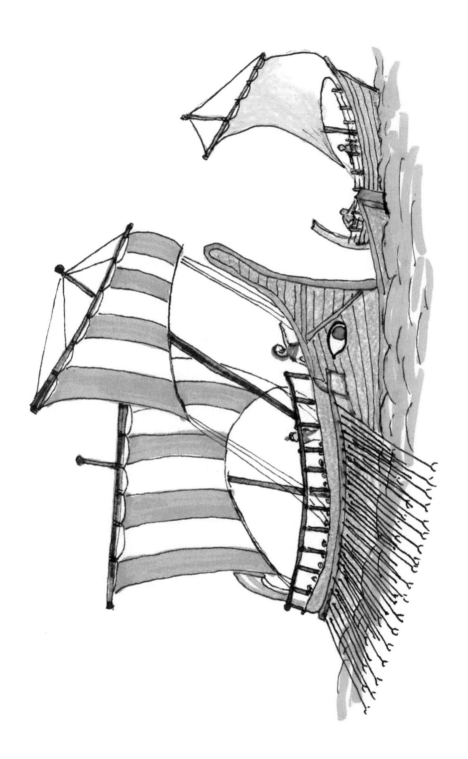

MOUNT OLYMPUS

The highest mountain in Greece is Mount Olympus, and also the home of the Greek gods. From the top, they could see most of Greece and the Aegean Sea. The twelve gods would meet there to talk about what help they could give mortals and what they wanted to do. Today this famous mountain is in a National Park.

Athena was a very clever goddess and helped the heroes and the people of Athens. She planted an Olive Tree on the Acropolis mountain in Athens and became their protector. Apollo was another god known for his healing and music. His sister, also a god, was Artemis. When she hunted, she used a silver bow and arrows. Aphrodite was known as the Goddess of Love and was very beautiful. She came from the island of Cyprus, and people said she loved Roses. Another god, Hermes, wore golden sandals and a golden helmet. Both had wings on them. He was the messenger of the Gods.

Elena: *"What did Athena plant on the Acropolis Mountain?"*

GREECE AND ROME

When the Romans came into contact with the ancient Greeks, all they wanted was money for the help and security the Romans offered to them. During these times, Rome was also in conflict with Carthage, which controlled much of the Mediterranean Sea. So the Romans asked for help from the Greeks as they were good shipbuilders and sailors. Between 31BC and 180AD, Greece became part of the Roman Empire. This allowed the City States to enjoy more peace and trade. The city of Athens flourished, and elite Greek citizens could even join the Roman Senate. Many Romans enjoyed visiting Greece and admired its art and culture. People from Greece and Rome began to speak both Greek and Latin. As contact between the Greeks and the Romans grew, a joint Roman and Greco empire formed. This brought about changes for children as they now had to learn more about the history and culture of both Greece and Rome.

Elena: *"What were the two languages people learned to speak?"*

GLOSSARY OF WORDS

Here are some words that Elena thinks you may wish to know and may help you to read this book.

- A Trireme was a large Greek Warship which had three banks of oars on each side. It also had a large Brass Ram on the front to help sink the enemy.
- Shields were used by the Greek soldiers. They were round-shaped and protected the soldiers from being injured.
- Markets were very busy places in the Greek towns where families went to buy and sell and meet their friends.
- Temples stood on the top of a hill so all the Greeks could easily see them; it was also where they went to pray to the Gods.
- Public buildings could be found in the town, like the Bathhouse and Temple and the town hall.
- Chariots were lightweight, small carts with two wheels which were moved using a horse.
- Gods and Goddesses lived in their temples, according to the ancient Greeks. They would go to the temples to talk to them and ask for their help.
- Heroes were special human beings with great supernatural powers, which gave them great strength to carry out their tasks.
- Clothes in Greece were made from lightweight materials, like tunics and dresses.
- Theatre was somewhere the Greeks loved to go. They watched plays and the actors who performed them in the theatres.
- Olympic Games were held every four years. It included many sports like wrestling, boxing, throwing the discus and throwing javelins. These games are still popular today with athletes.

ILLUSTRATIONS

Robbie Peterson created the illustrations in this book.

Elena: " *Can you tell me which illustration in the book you liked best?"*

ACKNOWLEDGMENT

To all the children in the entire world.

To all members past and present and fans of the Roman Living History Society the Antonine Guard which promotes the history of the Ancient World.

Permitte Divis Cetera

Ingram Content Group UK Ltd.
Milton Keynes UK
UKHW020606190523
422015UK00007B/15